PIONEERS IN HISTORY
EMPIRE BUILDERS

MICHAEL POLLARD

HEINEMANN CHILDREN'S REFERENCE
a division of Heinemann Educational Books Ltd
Halley Court, Jordan Hill, Oxford OX2 8EJ

OXFORD   LONDON   EDINBURGH
MELBOURNE   SYDNEY   AUCKLAND
MADRID   ATHENS   BOLOGNA
SINGAPORE   IBADAN   NAIROBI   HARARE
GABORONE   KINGSTON   PORTSMOUTH   NH(USA)

ISBN 0 431 00550 8

British Library Cataloguing in Publication Data
Pollard, Michael, 1931–
   The empire builders.
   1. Civilization, historyI
   I. Title   II. Series
909

Designed by Pardoe Blacker Limited
Picture research by Faith Perkins
Maps by Kevin Diaper

Printed in Hong Kong

91 92 93 94 95 10 9 8 7 6 5 4 3 2 1

Photographic credits

a = above b = below r = right l = left

The author and publishers wish to acknowledge, with
thanks, the following photographic sources:

The cover pictures are courtesy of The Bridgeman Art
Library and Peter Newark's Historical Pictures

Ancient Art & Architecture Collection pp11*a*, 19*a*, 24, 25*a*
and *b*, 26, 32; Bridgeman Art Library p37*a*; John Egan p22*b*;
Mary Evans Picture Library p33*a*; Robert Harding Picture
Library pp51*l*, 7*a*, 15*a*; John Hillelson © Dr Georg Gerster
p13*a*; Michael Holford pp5*r*, 6-7, 8*a* and *b*, 11*b*, 12, 13*b*, 15*b*,
16, 17*a* and *b*, 18, 21*b*, 22*a*, 30, 31*b*, 36, 37*b*; Hulton-Deutsche
Collection pp21*a*, 34; Hutchison Picture Library pp10, 28;
MacQuitty Collection p29; Mansell Collection p27*b*; Peter
Newark's Military Pictures pp35*a* and *b*; Ann and Bury
Peerless p31; Picturepoint pp7*b*, 19*b*; Scala pp23, 27*a*; South
American Pictures pp39*b* (Robert Francis), 40 (Tony
Morrison), 41*a* and *b* (Robert Francis), 43*a* (Tony Morrison);
Telegraph Colour Library p33*b*; Werner Forman Archive
pp39*a*, 42 (L Pigorini Museum, Rome), 43*b*.

The publishers have made every effort to trace the copyright
holders, but if they have inadvertently overlooked any,
they will be pleased to make the necessary arrangements at
the first opportunity.

Note to the reader
In this book there are some words in the text which are printed in **bold** type. This shows that the word is
listed in the glossary on page 46. The glossary gives a brief explanation of words which may be new to you.

Contents

Introduction

The first people who lived on Earth, thousands of years ago, were **nomads**, or wanderers. They moved about in groups, following herds of wild animals which they hunted for their meat and skins.

Gradually, some nomads began to change their way of life. They became farmers, which meant that they had to stay in one place to look after their crops and wait for the harvest.

The river lands

About 10000 years ago, people began to settle on the plains beside three rivers, the Nile, the Tigris and the Euphrates. The Nile flowed through the area of land which is now called Egypt, and the Tigris and Euphrates through the area which is now called Iraq. The river mud was very **fertile** and provided good farming land. The mud could also be shaped into bricks which were dried in the sun. Reeds growing on the river bank were also used to build houses. The people of the river lands settled down, built their homes and lived on their crops.

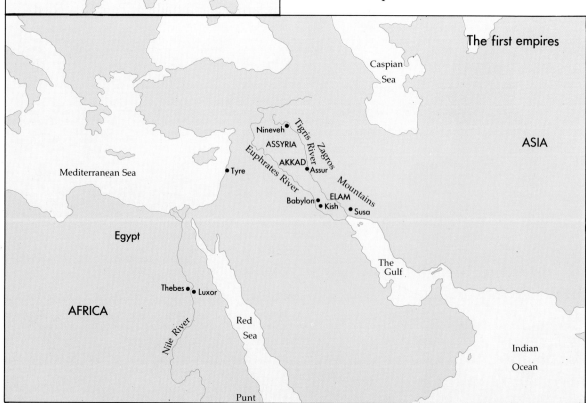

The first empires

▲ Marsh Arabs in southern Iraq today build their homes and boats from reeds just as the first settlers in Sumer did.

The farmers became very skilled. They dug ditches for irrigation, to take river water to the fields. They were able to work out the best time to plant corn and knew when it would be ready for harvesting. To help them with their calculations, they made the first calendar. They based this calendar on seasonal changes such as when leaves sprouted and when the Sun, Moon and stars changed their position in the sky. When the people began to produce more crops than they needed for their own use, some of them became merchants, travelling from place to place to **trade** their extra food for other goods.

▲ This gold and lapis lazuli statue of a goat was found at the Royal Cemetery in the Sumerian city of Ur. It dates from about 2500 BC.

The cities of Sumer

The settlers had to learn other skills as well as farming and trading. People needed to build houses, to make pottery, to spin yarn and weave cloth. Others worked with metal to make tools and ornaments. The goods were sold at markets, and villages grew up round those markets. About 3500 BC, at least five villages near the Tigris and Euphrates Rivers began to grow larger until they became cities.

These cities were situated in the area known as Sumer and their inhabitants, the Sumerians, formed the first **civilizations**. The Sumerians worked together as a group and obeyed the laws which were made by their rulers. It was not long, however, before the rulers quarrelled among themselves and the cities began a series of wars with one another.

For 3000 years, the cities of Sumer, and later those near the Nile River, were the most important in the western world. Their rulers were the first empire builders.

Sargon of Akkad

Archaeologists do not know as much about early civilizations as they would like to. They have to piece together the evidence from partly-ruined buildings, fragments of sculpture and metalwork, or perhaps from pictures and writing on stone and clay. Their answers may not always be correct, because often nothing is left of some of the places where the events took place, and few exact dates are known. So the information we have about the ruler of the world's first empire is incomplete.

▼ This decorated section from a musical instrument was found in the royal tomb of Ur in the 1920s. It shows the preparations for a feast.

The first empire builder

It is known that the first empire builder's name was Sargon, and that he was born in the city of Kish. Little else is known about his early life. About 2400 BC, Sargon moved to the land of Akkad, which was situated at a crossroads where the road between the Mediterranean Sea and The Gulf met the road coming north from the cities of Sumer. Since merchants had to pass through Akkad on their way to other places, Akkad became an important centre for trade. This was not enough for Sargon, he wanted to turn it into a centre of power as well.

The army of Akkad

When Sargon became king of Akkad in 2340 BC, he gathered together an army of 5000 skilled **warriors**. With them, he attacked and conquered his home city of Kish. Then he marched south to capture the other cities of Sumer one by one.

Sargon's next campaign was to invade the land of Elam, which lay to the north of The Gulf. Afterwards he turned west and his army fought their way to the Mediterranean Sea.

Sargon became ruler of all the land from the coast of the Mediterranean to the Zagros Mountains in the east. He called himself 'ruler of the four quarters of the world'.

▲ After the collapse of Akkad, Ur became powerful for a short time. The Ziggurat of Ur was built about 2100 BC. It consisted of platforms supporting a long staircase which led to a temple of the moon god.

▲ A copper head which is thought to be a portrait of Sargon of Akkad, one of the first empire builders.

Sargon gave his warriors an advantage over their enemies by sending them into battle well fed and well trained. Their methods of fighting also contributed to their success. They used bows and arrows and threw spears, whereas their enemies were used to hand to hand fighting with lances and heavy shields. Sargon's soldiers were also taught to creep up on their enemies and surprise them.

Sargon ruled his empire for about 50 years. It did not last long after he died, however, because it was difficult to rule such a large area of land, and Sargon had made many enemies. Akkad was attacked by tribes from the deserts and mountains, and by the year 2230 BC, the empire that Sargon had built had been destroyed.

Hammurabi of Babylon

The Akkad empire was destroyed because of its size. The ruler who **succeeded** Sargon could not keep in touch with all the different parts of the empire and so he lost control of it. The next great empire builder, Hammurabi of Babylon, made sure that he did not make the same mistake.

Babylon, beside the Euphrates River, was already an important city when Hammurabi became its ruler in 1792 BC. Hammurabi gained power over neighbouring cities by conquering them in battle. He invaded the land of Elam to the east of Babylon and took control of it. By the end of Hammurabi's reign in 1750 BC, he had made Babylon the centre of an empire.

The law-maker

Hammurabi believed that it was a king's duty to rule his people fairly, and to guard people's rights, even those of slaves. He made a set, or Code, of laws which were to be obeyed all over his empire, by rich and poor alike. There were nearly 300 laws, which dealt with crime and punishment, the buying and selling of goods, marriage and divorce, lending and borrowing money, the payment of wages, and many other matters of everyday life.

Stelae, which were pillars of stone with Hammurabi's Code of Laws carved on them, were set up in different parts of the empire so that everyone knew what the law said. One such stele was found by archaeologists in 1902, and this provided a great deal of information about life in Hammurabi's Babylon.

Hammurabi realized that he could not run his empire all by himself. He split it up into smaller areas run by local officials, whose duty was to ensure that the law was obeyed. Hammurabi often wrote to his officials, telling them how to do their work and reminding them to treat people fairly.

▼ The carving at the top of this stone stele shows Hammurabi receiving the Code of laws from the god Shamash. Below the carving are the laws of the Code.

Babylon's literature

Hammurabi's letters were writen on clay tablets, in a kind of picture-writing which used wedge-shaped marks called **cuneiform**. Hammurabi was interested in literature and made a collection of stories and poetry on clay tablets, which became the world's first library. While he was ruler of Babylon, legends about the people of the lands that made up the empire were written down, forming 'The Epic of Gilgamesh'.

The Gilgamesh stories were collected from many different places, and helped to make people content to be ruled from Babylon. They liked to think that they belonged to the same empire as the brave and adventurous Gilgamesh.

Long after Hammurabi died in 1750 BC, the people of Babylon continued to enjoy hearing the poems and stories in his library. They also continued to obey his laws, which although strict, were fair to everyone.

▲ A scene from 'The Epic of Gilgamesh' which described the adventures of the hero, Gilgamesh, in his search for the secret of life and death.

▲ A cuneiform tablet from Babylon which was used to teach geometry around 1800 BC.

Hatshepsut, queen of Egypt

The second great civilization in the Middle East began beside the Nile River in Egypt about 5000 years ago. Every summer, the Nile flooded, and when the flood water went down, it left behind thick black mud. This made good farming land, so fertile that two or even three crops could be grown on it each year. There was too much food for the Egyptians to eat themselves, and they started to sell it.

Farming made the Egyptians wealthy and they began to build an empire by trade instead of war. They traded with people in lands across the Mediterranean Sea, in East Africa and in southern Asia. Their empire stretched southwards along the Nile Valley and northwards along the eastern shore of the Mediterranean Sea.

▼ These crops are being grown on fertile farming land on the west bank of the Nile River in Egypt.

Besides being skilled farmers and traders, the Egyptians became good at building, writing and painting. They enjoyed music and dancing.

A powerful queen

In 1503 BC, Hatshepsut became queen of Egypt. Hatshepsut rejected warfare as a means of gaining power, and wanted to rule over an empire that traded peacefully with other countries. She ordered an **expedition** to go to the land that the Egyptians called Punt. This was on the African coast at the southern end of the Red Sea that is now known as Ethiopia and Djibouti.

The expedition involved a long sea journey down the Red Sea, and the Egyptians built eight ships especially for the journey. They set sail in 1492 BC, taking

with them weapons and other goods to exchange. They also took gifts for the leaders of Punt to show that they had come in peace.

The people of Punt welcomed the Egyptian sailors and the goods they brought with them. In return, the Egyptians received gold, myrrh, ebony, baboons and animals' skins. Myrrh is a gum taken from myrrh trees and it was used to make perfume, incense and medicine. The Egyptians were also given living myrrh trees, which could not be obtained in Egypt. Queen Hatshepsut wanted these trees to plant in front of the temple she had had built.

▲ The temple that was built for Queen Hatshepsut to celebrate the events of her reign. The Egyptian rulers believed that they needed to remind the gods of their good deeds.

▼ Part of a wall painting in Queen Hatshepsut's temple telling the story of the expedition to Punt. The figures are shown holding gifts of herbs and olive branches.

Hatshepsut's temple

The Egyptians believed in many gods, and Egyptian kings and queens built huge temples to their gods near the main city of Thebes. Since the fertile river land was too valuable to build on, the temples were built at the edge of the desert.

Queen Hatshepsut's temple, which can still be seen near the town of Luxor, was one of the most beautiful. It has stone carvings that tell the story of her reign in pictures and a whole gallery of carvings showing both the voyage to Punt and Hatshepsut welcoming the sailors on their return.

Hatshepsut was queen for over 20 years, and the end of her reign is a mystery. When she died in 1482 BC, her stepson Thutmose III became king, and some historians believe that he murdered his stepmother. Certainly he hated her, since during his reign he had her face chipped away from all the pictures in her temple.

The Assyrians

◄ This is one of the carvings that Ashurbanipal ordered for his palace at Nineveh. He is shown hunting on horseback.

The Tigris River flows down from the mountains of Turkey through a hilly district called Assur. About 5000 years ago, people began to settle in the Assur hills, and became known as the Assyrians. The first Assyrian settlers provided food for themselves by farming the land around them. However, they soon found that they lacked timber and metal so they gradually began to trade for these. The Assyrians became known as successful traders.

Early battles fought by the Assyrians were usually to defend the borders of their valuable agricultural land. Then, in about 1350 BC, the Assyrian king, Ashur-Uballit I turned to conquest as a means of gaining power. He called himself 'Great King', and is thought to be the first of the Assyrian empire builders.

The Assyrians built up a powerful, well-trained and well-equipped army. It had lancers on horseback, and bowmen on foot, on horseback and in horse-drawn chariots. The soldiers wore pointed metal helmets and armour to protect their legs, and carried shields. When necessary, the Assyrians could put as many as 100000 soldiers against their enemies.

Finally, the Assyrians used the weapon of fear itself. They fiercely punished their enemies and the people who rebelled against them as a warning to others.

By about 730 BC, the Assyrians had conquered Babylon. At this time they also made Nineveh, in their own district of Assur, into their chief, or capital, city. They made it into a fine city with its own piped water supply and roads linking it with the places that the Assyrians had conquered.

Ashurbanipal the empire builder

In 668 BC, Ashurbanipal became king of Assyria, and decided to make the Assyrian empire even larger and stronger. His army went on the march, first capturing Tyre on the Mediterranean coast, then advancing into Egypt. After that they turned east, and captured Susa, the capital city of Elam.

The story of Ashurbanipal's conquests was told on stone slabs covered with carvings that the king had made for his palace at Nineveh. The slabs also told of what followed each conquest. The defeated enemy soldiers were subjected to torture, starvation and death.

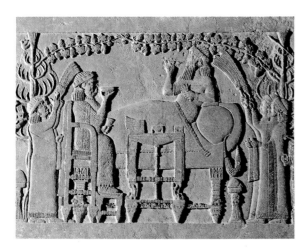

▲ King Ashurbanipal resting after his conquest of Elam while servants bring him food and wine. His queen is sitting opposite him.

▼ An aerial view of the city of Nineveh. It was the capital of Assyria from 880 to 707 BC. About 80 000 people lived in the city.

Ashurbanipal was not only interested in war. At Nineveh he built up a library of over 25 000 clay tablets. Some had poetry and stories carved on them, others told all that the Assyrians knew about science and health.

The fall of Nineveh

Ashurbanipal was Assyria's last empire builder. Soon after he died in 627 BC, rebels inside the empire and enemies outside attacked the Assyrians. One by one their cities were destroyed, until in 614 BC, enemy armies surrounded Nineveh. The Assyrians held out bravely, but after two years they had to surrender. Nineveh was burned to the ground and its inhabitants were either killed or taken as slaves. The Assyrian empire had come to an end.

Darius, king of Persia

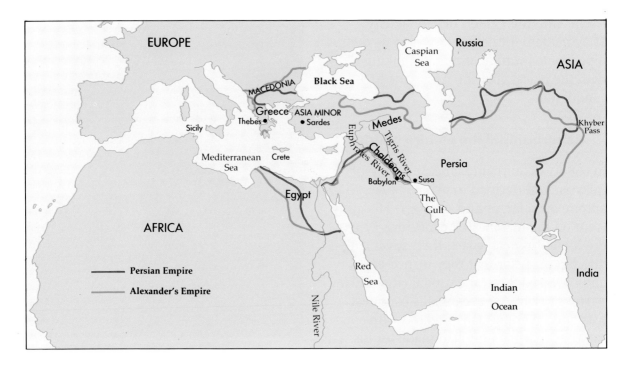

The tribes whose armies defeated the Assyrians were the Chaldeans, the Medes and the Persians. The Chaldeans came from southern Babylonia, and the Medes and Persians both came from the country which is now called Iran. The Persians started to build up their own empire, and by 530 BC it had become the largest in the world. Its first emperor was King Cyrus II the Great, who was killed in battle in 529 BC.

A man called Gaumata then became king but his claim to the throne was soon challenged. Darius, the son of one of Cyrus's governors, thought he had a stronger claim to be king. One night in 521 BC, Darius and six of his friends attacked a fort where Gaumata was staying and killed him. Darius made himself king and called himself 'Great King, King of Kings'.

Organizing the empire

Many people would not accept Darius as king at first, and it was years before there was peace. Even when the Persian empire was at peace, its great size made it difficult to control. It extended from the Greek islands to the borders of India and up into southern Russia. As king, Darius had to find a way of ruling it properly.

Darius divided the empire into 20 parts called **satraps**, each with its own governor. He sent men to spy on the governors, to make sure they were carrying out his orders. His spies were told to be 'the eyes and ears of the king'.

Each of the satraps had to provide troops for Darius's army, and workers to build roads to link the different parts of the

14

empire to one another. The main road across the empire was called the 'royal road'. It was 2700 kilometres long and ran from Sardes near the Aegean coast all the way to Susa near The Gulf, where the royal palace was located. Messengers riding in **relays** could travel from one end of the road to the other in five days.

Darius knew that a system of roads would make trade easier throughout the empire, and he also improved sea routes. A canal had been started some centuries earlier, between the Nile River and the Red Sea, and Darius had it repaired and completed so that it could be used by ships trading between Persia and Egypt.

▲ Darius stayed at different palaces in his empire depending on the time of year. The ruins of the palace at Persepolis can still be seen today.

▼ A Persian archer, one of 2000 soldiers which Darius had under his command.

A free empire

The tribes who lived on the borders of the Persian empire sometimes rebelled against their ruler. This meant that Darius had to fight many small wars on the borders of his empire. He was not really a warlike man, however. He was more interested in running the empire well. Unlike the Assyrian kings, he did not punish the people who had been his enemies. They were allowed to go on worshipping their own gods, and they were given their freedom as long as they paid their **taxes**.

Darius was a peaceful ruler and his **tolerant** ideas helped to unite the Persian empire. However, after his death in 486 BC, fighting began again. The Persians went to war with the Greeks, who became the next empire builders.

15

The Greek cities

◀ The remains of a Greek colony on the island of Sicily, the largest island in the Mediterranean Sea.

Greece is a **peninsula**, which means that it has a long coastline on three sides and a border with Europe to the north. The island of Crete is to the south in the Mediterranean Sea, and there are many islands to the east. Inland, Greece has high mountains and deep valleys. Travel by sea was easier than by land, so the ancient Greeks usually built their cities in valleys near the coast. These cities were small, since there was little land on which to build, but each was a **city state**. Each city state was run by its own **government**.

Not all Greeks took part in running the city states. The Greeks believed that some men were only fit to be slaves. Women, who did most of the hard work, especially in the farms, were not allowed to be **citizens**. They were also not expected to think deeply about subjects such as science and the arts, which were thought to be interesting only to men.

Settling abroad

About 750 BC, the cities became very crowded, because there was not enough land around them to allow them to become bigger. The Greeks had to find somewhere else to live, so they set up new cities along the northern shores of the Mediterranean and the Black Sea.

These new cities were called **colonies**. Each one was a city state in its own right, modelled on the 'mother city' that had provided the colony with money and leaders. Some of the new cities were built on land which was good for farming. Others became trading cities with busy ports.

By about 500 BC, there were many Greek city states both within Greece and abroad. There was never a Greek empire with one single ruler. However, the Greeks all spoke the same language, shared the same ideas and worshipped the same gods.

The Olympic Games

Sometimes the Greek cities and colonies fought amongst themselves. There was one event every four years, however, that always brought the Greeks together. This was the Olympiad, and even if the Greeks were fighting each other, they stopped for three months so that they could take part in it.

The Olympiad was a festival of sport held in the stadium at Olympia. Any Greek citizen could take part, which meant that women were excluded. There were races of 200, 400 and 5000 metres as well as wrestling, boxing, chariot races, horse-racing and long-jumping. There were also throwing competitions, in which men competed to see how far they could throw the discus, a solid metal disc, and the javelin, a light spear.

▲ A Greek vase showing runners in a long distance race.

▼ The Greeks built a fleet of merchant ships to trade between their colonies.

17

Alexander the Great

Alexander III was an empire builder who earned himself the title 'Alexander the Great'. He was a powerful general who built an empire that covered almost all the known eastern parts of the world, including the Persian empire and stretching as far east as India.

Alexander was born in 356 BC, the son of King Philip II of Macedonia, a country to the north east of Greece. Philip II was a powerful king, who conquered the Greek city states and brought them together under his rule.

When Philip was murdered, the Greeks thought that this meant the end of Macedonian rule, and the city of Thebes rebelled against Alexander, the new king. Alexander, who was 20 years old at this time, led his army to Thebes and destroyed the city. Many of its people were killed and the rest were taken as slaves. After that, no other Greek cities dared to fight the new king.

Europe's first empire

It soon became Alexander's ambition to conquer the powerful Persian empire. He collected a huge army. His main striking force was made up of 5000 cavalry which were so good in battle that he hardly ever had to use his infantry force of 3000 men.

In 334 BC, Alexander led his soldiers against the armies of the Persian empire. Over the next two years, Alexander conquered Asia Minor, defeating Darius III, then went on to conquer Egypt. Once this was done, he marched east to conquer Babylon and Susa. Wherever the army went, Macedonian governors followed, to help Alexander to rule his new empire.

Through his conquests, Alexander became king of Persia, and grew to love the country. He wore Persian clothes, married a Persian princess, and it became his ambition to unite Greece and Persia in one empire. He encouraged his soldiers to marry Persian women by giving them large **dowries**, or payments, and many Persian soldiers joined Alexander's army.

▲ A Roman bronze statuette of Alexander the Great on horseback. Alexander was a skilled horseman, and part of his great success in battle was due to his skilful control of his team of cavalry soldiers.

◀ Alexander the Great dressed as emperor of Persia.

The last march

Now Alexander wanted to conquer the lands to the east of Persia. He hoped to reach the end of the world so that he could call himself 'King of the world'.

▼ The ancient Greek city of Ephesus was one of the cities which were freed from the Persians by Alexander the Great in 333 BC.

In 330 BC, Alexander began his last march, which took him across deserts and mountains as far as northern India. His army won every battle against the tribes that opposed them. At one point, Alexander sent some of his soldiers over the famous Khyber Pass that leads into India. At last the march came to a halt, because the army mutinied and refused to go any further. Many of Alexander's men had been away from home for more than ten years.

Alexander agreed to turn back if they went home a different way. He sent some by sea on a voyage of exploration along The Gulf, and led the rest back to Babylon by land.

Alexander's next plan was to lead an army along the north coast of Africa, but in 323 BC he fell ill and died before he could begin the march. He was only 33 years old. In the short 12 years of Alexander's reign he had built a huge empire and founded over 70 cities.

19

The Carthaginians

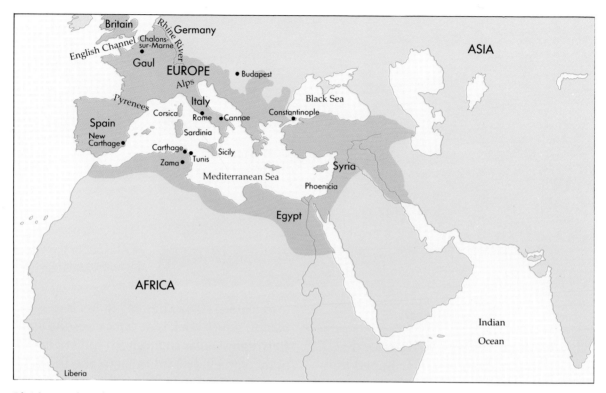

If Alexander the Great had not died, his next conquest was likely to have been Carthage in North Africa. The sailors and merchants of Carthage had built up a trading empire that covered North Africa, part of Spain, Sardinia and Corsica. Carthage also controlled the sea routes of the western Mediterranean Sea.

Carthage was founded about 800 BC. The people of Phoenicia, which is now called Lebanon, were seafarers who set up many colonies far from their homeland. Carthage was one of these colonies.

When Phoenicia was conquered by the Persians, Carthage was far enough away to stay free. It became a great trading port. About 8000 years ago Carthage was setting up its own colonies and building an empire.

War at sea

Ships from Carthage sailed to Spain and Sicily where colonies were begun. One expedition explored the west coast of Africa as far south as Liberia. The Carthaginians were more interested in buying and selling than in fighting, and wherever they went they set up trading stations. The merchants of Carthage became very wealthy, and wanted to keep all the trade in the western Mediterranean Sea to themselves. However, the merchants' ships were wide and heavy which meant that they could only move slowly. They were sometimes attacked by pirates. The Carthaginians were good shipbuilders as well as sailors, and they learned to build

20

► The ancient city and harbour of Carthage. Archaeologists use evidence from excavations to reconstruct how a place may have looked in the past.

fast warships to protect their merchant fleet.

By 500 BC, Rome had become powerful. The Romans began to object to Carthage having colonies so close to Italy in Sicily, Sardinia and Corsica. At first the rulers of Rome agreed not to interfere with Carthaginian trade, because they knew they were incapable of winning a war against Carthage. Rome had neither warships nor the skills to design and build them. However, all this changed when the Romans found a wrecked Carthaginian warship and used its design to build warships of their own. They even improved on the Carthaginian ship by adding a boarding-bridge so that soldiers could cross from their own ship to the enemy's. Rome was ready to fight Carthage.

War broke out between Rome and Carthage in 264 BC. The Romans drove the Carthaginians out of Sicily, then defeated them in a battle at sea.

War in Africa

In 256 BC, a Roman army landed in Africa and built a strong base there. The following year the Romans marched on the city of Tunis, only a few kilometres from Carthage.

The Carthaginians gathered a large army together and equipped it with both cavalry and elephants. The elephants charged the enemy, frightening the soldiers and their horses. The elephants could also carry archers and spearmen on their backs.

After the battle of Tunis the defeated Romans left Africa. On the way back to Italy their ships were caught in a storm and many soldiers drowned. Another fleet of warships was built, but these too were destroyed. However, in 241 BC, the Romans completely defeated the Carthaginians at sea, and both sides agreed to peace.

▼ Carthaginian warships were copies of Phoenician longships. They had sails and oars and strengthened bows so that they could ram enemy ships.

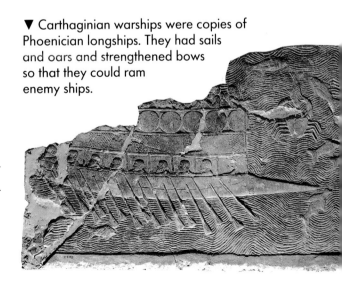

Hannibal's march to Italy

▲ On this silver coin, Hannibal wears a laurel wreath on his head to show that he is a hero.

Although peace was made between Rome and Carthage after the Carthaginians were defeated at sea, the peace did not last long. Carthage started a **campaign**, or planned series of battles, to bring the whole of Spain into its empire, and they built a city there called New Carthage. The Romans did not want to see Carthage become more powerful, and they threatened war. They organized one army to go to Spain and one to go to Africa.

The young general called Hannibal who now commanded the Carthaginian army decided that he would have to attack Rome before the Romans attacked Carthage. Before the Roman armies were even aboard their ships, Hannibal was on the march. He planned to surprise the Romans by advancing into Italy from the north, over the high mountains called the Alps.

Across the mountains

Hannibal's army of 50 000 infantry, 9000 cavalry and 37 war elephants set out on its march of over 2500 kilometres in 218 BC. They crossed the mountains of the Pyrenees on their way out of Spain, passed through southern Gaul where they were attacked by hostile tribes, until at last they reached the Alps. Hannibal had been marching slowly, because he did not want the Romans to recognize his plan. As a result, the march had taken six months and by this time winter was starting.

Hannibal's men were all used to the climate of warmer countries and found it difficult to climb on snow and ice. Some slipped and had to be left where they had fallen. Others fell ill, and a number of soldiers froze to death. When Hannibal at last reached Italy, he had lost half his army.

▼ The Alps extend over 1000 kilometres from France to Yugoslavia.

Victory and defeat

In spite of their losses, it seemed that nothing could stop Hannibal's soldiers on their march south to Rome. The Romans fought Hannibal's army in three battles and each time Hannibal won.

At last, a Roman army of about 86000 men gathered at Cannae in south Italy, in the summer of 216 BC. Hannibal had about 50000 men altogether, but some of them were new, inexperienced recruits.

When the battle started, the centre of the Roman army began to advance. Hannibal ordered his soldiers in the centre to fall back, and the Romans pressed forward, believing they were winning.

Then the two flanks, or sides, of Hannibal's army closed in behind the Roman army and trapped it. Of the huge army that had come to fight, only 36000 were left alive. The Carthaginians, however, had lost only 500 men.

Hannibal stayed in Italy for 15 years, defending the land he had gained from attacks by the Romans. Then he was called back to Carthage because a Roman army had invaded Africa. In 202 BC, Hannibal and the Roman general Scipio met at Zama, not far from the city of Carthage.

There were 80 elephants in the front line of the Carthaginian army, but this time they caused disaster. When the Roman trumpets sounded to start the battle, the elephants turned around and stampeded into their own troops. Seeing Hannibal's men in trouble, Scipio led his soldiers round to the back of Hannibal's army and attacked from behind. Hannibal had to surrender and ask for peace, in the only defeat of his career. With this victory over the Carthaginians, Rome had won final control of the western Mediterranean Sea.

▼ Hannibal's war elephants carried archers protected by wooden battlements. They were like small castles on the move.

The Roman empire

By 60 BC, the Roman empire included almost all the land around the Mediterranean Sea. The tribes that had been conquered did not want to be ruled by the Romans, and the Romans had to struggle to keep control. This task was complicated by the way in which Rome was governed. Rome was a **republic** ruled by its people through an assembly of noblemen. This assembly, called the **senate,** elected two leaders and those leaders often quarrelled, causing confusion and disunity in the senate and among the people ruled by it.

Then in 60 BC, a strong leader, Julius Caesar, aimed to end this confusion. He persuaded two others to share the rule of the empire with him, and they became the First **Triumvirate**.

The Romans ruled their empire by dividing it into sections of land called provinces, each with its own governor. Julius Caesar governed part of a province called Gaul, which is now the country called France. It was only southern Gaul, however, and tribes from further north often attacked the Romans. Caesar decided to stop this by conquering the rest of Gaul.

To war with Gaul

Caesar stayed in Gaul for almost ten years. His well-trained and well-equipped army fought and defeated the **Gallic** tribes one by one. Caesar marched his army north until they reached the English Channel between Gaul and Britain. At its narrowest, the Channel is only 30 kilometres wide, and Caesar thought he would add Britain to the Roman empire.

His first invasion in 55 BC was a failure, but he returned in 54 BC, with several hundred ships and 30 000 men. They marched through south eastern England for about 150 kilometres. The Britons fought them in chariots and on foot, but they could not defeat the Roman army with its better weapons. They quickly made peace.

◀ Julius Caesar was a strong-willed leader who changed the government of Rome from a republic into a dictatorship.

Caesar could not stay to make Britain a Roman province, because some of the Gallic tribes had rebelled against Roman rule. He returned to Gaul to fight them again, and it was three years before they were back under control. He also had to fight the German tribes, who invaded Gaul across the Rhine River.

The rivals

While Caesar was fighting in Gaul, there had been changes in the rest of the empire. The people of Syria had fought the Romans and won, and the Roman governor of Syria had been killed. This left just two leaders again, Julius Caesar and his rival Pompey. Pompey and the senate were jealous of Caesar, and wanted him to give up his control of the army. Caesar refused, and **civil war** broke out in 49 BC between the two leaders and their followers.

▲ Legions of the Roman army could march along the expertly-built Roman roads in columns which were six soldiers wide.

▲ Marcus Brutus was one of the leaders of the plot to assassinate Julius Caesar in 44 BC.

Pompey was defeated, and fled to Egypt, where he was murdered. After this, Caesar had to defeat rebellions which took place in North Africa and in Spain.

In 46 BC, Caesar returned to Rome as its only ruler, but his rule did not last long. There was a plot to get rid of Caesar, and in 44 BC he was stabbed to death. After Caesar's murder, the Second Triumvirate, which included his great-nephew Octavian, began to rule Rome.

In AD43, the Romans made another attempt to invade Britain and make it a Roman province. This time they were successful, and Britain was to remain part of the Roman empire for the next 400 years.

25

Attila the Hun

The Roman empire never stretched as far as the plains and forests of eastern Europe. These areas were inhabited, or lived in, by tribes which the Romans called 'barbarians'. They used this name to describe people who were neither Roman nor Greek.

One of the barbarian tribes, the Huns, had settled in southern Russia and the country which is now called Hungary. The earliest Huns were herders, looking after their animals and living in small farming villages. They were also fierce fighters, feared by all who knew them.

Attila's conquests

By the time Attila became their king, in AD 434, the Huns had already fought and conquered a number of small kingdoms. Some rulers were so afraid of the Huns'

terrifying reputation that they gave in without a struggle, and paid tribute straightaway. Tribute was the name given to the money or goods which had to be paid by a defeated kingdom to the conquering power.

Attila set up his court in the place which is now Budapest, and ordered raids to continue on the other tribes of central Europe. His raiders brought back news of other countries. They described the rich, fertile land of Gaul and the wealth of Constantinople and Rome. Attila began to dream of conquering the whole of Europe.

Over a hundred years before Attila had come to power, the Roman empire had been divided into two parts. The eastern half was ruled from Constantinople and the western half from Rome. In AD 447, Attila attacked the eastern Roman empire. Although he failed to conquer Constantinople, the eastern Romans had to pay tribute to Attila and lost some of their land to him. Attila now gathered together an army to attack the western empire.

The march to Gaul

Attila began marching in AD 451 at the head of 70000 soldiers and their families. It is thought that his plan was to conquer Gaul and settle the Huns there.

The Huns were not a trained army like the Romans. As they marched, they raided

◀ Attila's cruel and savage reputation spread terror throughout Europe.

every village they came to. They looted the houses, robbing them of everything, then burned the village down. The people who were not killed fled in terror.

The Roman army planned to defeat the Huns by joining forces with the army of the German tribe called Visigoths. They met the Huns somewhere near Chalons-sur-Marne in what is now north eastern France. In a battle that lasted all day, thousands were killed on both sides, including the Visigoth king. At last, in the only defeat of his reign, Attila had to **retreat** and withdraw his army. The Huns returned to their own country.

In AD 452, Attila and his army attempted to invade Italy. This time, rather than being conquered in battle, they were defeated by a famine which was sweeping the country. The army advanced into the north of Italy, but they were driven back by hunger and the invasion failed.

The following year, Attila planned to attack the eastern Roman empire once more, but he died before he could do so. After Attila's death, there was no one powerful enough to control the Huns' empire, and it soon became divided.

▲ The Huns' attempt to invade Italy led to a confrontation between Attila and Pope Leo I.

▼ Under Attila's leadership, his army of Huns covered long distances on their powerful horses.

Asian civilizations

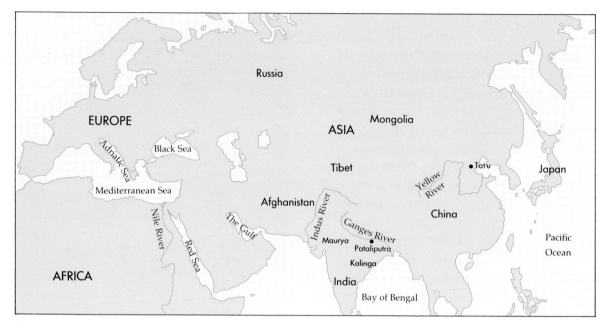

The early civilizations that began around the Mediterranean Sea were not the only ones in the world at that time. Thousands of kilometres to the east of the Mediterranean Sea lies the continent of Asia. It is a vast area of mountains, deserts, and great plains called steppes. Fierce winds blow across Asia, and it is very cold in winter on the areas of high ground.

The first people who lived in Asia had a hard life. Few crops could be grown, so they had to hunt wild animals for food. They were nomads, because they had to keep moving from place to place to find fresh supplies of food.

The mountain streams flow down to become rivers like the Yellow River in China, and the Indus River in India. Where these rivers reach the sea there are wide plains of fertile mud. Some nomads settled on these plains and became farmers.

▼ A rice paddy field in Bengal. Today, farmers in northern India still use water from the Ganges River to irrigate their crops.

The Yellow River

The first civilization in Asia lived on the banks of the Yellow River in China. People began to settle there about 7000 years ago, in villages surrounded by walls shaped out of pressed earth. At the same time, people were starting to settle beside the Nile River in Egypt. By about 6000 years ago, the Chinese had learned how to **irrigate** their land by using water from the Yellow River. Some parts of the irrigation system they invented are still used today.

By 1500 BC, some of the villages had grown into cities. The most important of these was ruled by the Shang **dynasty** or line of kings. Although they were farmers, the Shang grew rich by trading. The Shang had large chariot armies of as many as 5000 men. With these armies, the Shang raided and conquered the surrounding cities until they ruled over a large kingdom around the Yellow River.

Early Indian civilizations

About 4500 years ago, there were villages in the valley of the Indus River in north west India. Some of these villages became cities which were very advanced for their time. They were well laid out, and many houses had both bathrooms and private wells.

These cities formed the Indus Valley civilization. It lasted for several centuries and no one really knows why it came to an end. It is thought that there may have been an invasion from the north.

The invaders were probably Aryans who came across the mountains from central Asia. The Aryans were not used to city life

▲ The ruined city of Mohenjo-Daro in the Indus valley. It was once a major trading centre.

and did not understand it, so the cities of the Indus valley fell into ruins. The irrigation systems that had been built became blocked and useless, because the Aryans were interested in rearing cattle, rather than in growing grain.

Since cattle need fresh grass to graze on, the Aryans moved on with their herds. They travelled eastwards, across northern India, until they reached the valley of the Ganges River.

The people of the Ganges had discovered how to make iron and how to heat it to shape it into weapons and tools. The weapons made them powerful, and the tools made them more successful farmers. The people of the Ganges wanted to defend themselves and their land from the Aryan invaders, and used their weapons to do so.

The empire of Ashoka

◄ This stone sculpture of the Buddha preaching was made between 300 and 200 BC. In ruling his empire, Ashoka followed the principles of the Buddhist faith.

empire that reached right across northern India. It included the river valleys of the Ganges and Indus, and stretched into the mountains of Afghanistan.

Ashoka continued to make war against the Indian cities and kingdoms that did not belong to his empire. The last to surrender to Ashoka was Kalinga, in what is now Bengal. Once that country had been conquered, Ashoka was ruler of all India except for the southern tip. He realized that it would be difficult to keep an empire of this size under his control. It would have taken a huge army to rule the Mauryan empire by force, since the people spoke many different languages and followed many religions. Ashoka tried to rule it another way.

Prince of Peace

There had been fierce battles when Ashoka's army had conquered Kalinga. Over 100 000 people had been killed, and another 15 000 had been taken prisoner. Although the army had been carrying out Ashoka's orders, he was shocked at the violent outcome. Ashoka decided to reject violence as a way of controlling people, and began to study religion instead. He became a Buddhist. One belief that Buddhists hold is that it is wrong to kill any living thing, no matter how small.

After Alexander the Great retreated from India in 326 BC, the small kingdoms of India started to fight among themselves. Finally, the kingdom of Maurya gained power over all the other kingdoms. The capital city of Maurya was Pataliputra, now called Patna, on the Ganges River. In 272 BC, Ashoka became king of Maurya and ruler of an

Ashoka's life changed completely. He began to believe in the importance of peace, calling himself 'the Prince of Peace'. He had his new beliefs carved on stone columns which were placed all over his empire. Many of these columns can still be seen today. The inscriptions or words carved on them show that Ashoka believed in ruling his people by reasoning with them rather than by making them obey his orders.

'All men are my children', he said. He told his people to 'flee from evil and do good, to be loving, true, patient and pure in life'. Although Ashoka was a Buddhist, he respected other religions and allowed his people to follow them if they wanted to.

▲ Ashoka built the Great Stupa at Sanchi in northern India. The ashes of Buddha were buried beneath it, so Buddhists came to worship there.

▼ The top of one of Ashoka's stone columns which were built in the main cities of his empire. Carved messages on them set out his wish to rule his people in peace.

Rule by agreement

Since Ashoka did not have a large army to feed and clothe and equip with weapons, all the empire's money could be spent to help its people. The elderly and the sick were cared for, whether they were poor or rich. Ashoka had good roads built, with trees along them to give shade for travellers and their animals, and rest-houses for overnight shelter. Wells were dug to bring water to villages which had none, with reservoirs to store water for the dry season.

Ashoka's empire did not last long after he died in 232 BC, because there was no one powerful enough to take his place in his peaceful empire. Warring tribes from outside soon took over. Ashoka himself, however, is still remembered in India today as a good and wise ruler.

The Great Wall of China

In the same way that the Mauryan kingdom became leader among the warring Indian states, so the Ch'in state came to rule over China. The people of Ch'in were fierce warriors, who killed everyone they captured. People from the other Chinese states called them 'the wild beasts of Ch'in'.

By 221 BC, the Ch'in had conquered the whole of China. In that year the Ch'in ruler gave himself the title Ch'in Shih Huang Ti, which means 'First Emperor of the Ch'in'. From then on, 'Ch'in' meant the whole of China. It also meant 'the world', for the Chinese knew nothing about the rest of the world outside China.

▼ The Great Wall of China follows the shape of the countryside across which it was built. Shih Huang Ti ordered the wall to be built to protect his empire from invasion by raiders from the north.

The making of China

Shih Huang Ti decided that he was the first Chinese ruler in history and that his way of ruling was best. In 213 BC, he ordered the destruction of all writings which disagreed with his opinions and all those which described the past.

Before Shih Huang Ti had become emperor, China had been divided into several states. This meant that a number of different languages were both spoken and written, and ways of weighing and measuring also varied from one state to another. Shih Huang Ti made laws which ordered that only one language and one set of weights and measures should be used throughout his empire. He even made a law which ruled how wide carts should be. Anyone who did not obey these laws was put to death.

Under Shih's rule, slaves were treated badly. Many were worked so hard that they died. Slaves built roads and drained marshes. They built a huge palace for Shih in his capital city, Xian. Over 300 000 slaves helped to build Shih's most famous work, the Great Wall of China.

The north west of China was often raided by tribes from the mountains. Lengths of wall, made of beaten earth, had been built in the past to keep the raiders out. Shih decided to link the lengths of wall together to make one long wall. It took 20 years to build, and when it was finished it was 2400 kilometres long. The Great Wall of China was the largest piece of building work ever completed, and it can still be seen today.

◀ Shih Huang Ti ordered that all books should be destroyed except those on law, horticulture and herbal medicine. Authors were also killed.

The terracotta army

Shih wanted to live forever, and the only thing he was afraid of was death. He had soldiers around him to protect him wherever he went, and he felt he needed an army around him when he died. Slaves built him a large tomb with a dome-shaped roof painted to look like the sky at night. It was guarded by over 7500 life-size models of soldiers, made of a type of clay called terracotta. These models were only discovered in 1974, and some of them have since been put on show. This collection of life-size model soldiers is sometimes called the 'terracotta army'.

Shih had been such a harsh ruler that few Chinese were sorry when he died in 210 BC. Soon afterwards, the slaves and the army rose against the Ch'in royal family and put their own leader in power.

▲ Shih Huang Ti's 'terracotta army'.

The Mongol empire

The high, flat land of Mongolia lies to the north of China. Most of southern Mongolia is desert, but the steppe country in the north with its wide treeless plains has good grazing land. The early Mongolian people were nomadic herders, driving their flocks from one pasture to another. They were also skilled horseriders and warriors.

There were a number of clans or tribes in Mongolia, each with its own 'khan' or leader, and they all fought against one another. In 1180, a 13-year-old boy called Temujin became khan of his tribe when his father was killed. Within a few years, Temujin and his warriors had fought and conquered the other tribes one by one, until they had created a united Mongolia. In 1206 Temujin was given the title Genghis Khan, meaning 'universal ruler'.

▼ Mounted Mongol troops crossing a frozen river.

The unbeatable army

Genghis Khan believed that he should be ruler of the whole world. To make this aim come true, he built up a large and powerful army. The Mongol army was successful because it could move very fast on foot and on horseback, it had better weapons than its enemies, and it was extremely well trained. Genghis Khan had made a code of laws, some of which were about the training of his army. Even in peacetime, for example, men had to practise archery skills by hunting wild animals.

The Mongols attacked China first. They forced their way across the Great Wall, and the Chinese emperor soon surrendered. Genghis Khan turned next to southern Russia and the lands of the old Russian empire.

The Mongols made sure that the terrible news of their coming went before them. It was known that the Mongols were never

▲ Genghis Khan's army capturing a Chinese town. The event is recorded in this Persian miniature from the 1500s.

Khan and emperor

One of the most famous descendents of Genghis Khan was his grandson, Kublai Khan, who became khan in 1260. Kublai was quite unlike his grandfather. Although he continued the Mongol conquest of China, leading his army further south, Kublai Khan did not kill the Chinese leaders as the Mongols had always done. He listened to them and learned from them, because he admired the Chinese way of life.

When Kublai Khan became emperor of the whole of China, he made the city of Tatu, now Beijing, his capital. He was a good ruler and greatly improved the way China was run. Laws were made and carried out, hospitals were built for the sick, and traders and travellers were made welcome.

Even before Kublai Khan's death in 1294, some parts of the Mongol empire were already being ruled as separate small kingdoms. Not long afterwards, the rest of the Mongol empire began to split up. The Mongols' dream of ruling the world was over.

satisfied until every one of their enemies was dead. The Mongol army was also known to use heavy catapults and battering rams to break down city walls, and to use bombs and rockets containing gunpowder. Fear made many leaders surrender rather than fight, and the Mongol empire grew rapidly.

Before Genghis Khan died in 1227, he named his son Ogedai as his successor. On becoming khan, Ogedai sent out armies to make more conquests. At one point the Mongol empire stretched as far west as the Adriatic Sea and as far east as the Pacific coast of China, and extended northwards into Russia. When Ogedai himself died in 1241, however, the Mongols retreated from Europe, never to return.

▶ Kublai Khan opened up trade and communication links between China and Europe.

The Moghuls in India

The Mongols who stayed on in the old Persian empire were called 'Moghuls' by the Persians. The Moghuls became followers of Islam, the religion which was founded by the **prophet** Mohammed. One of the military leaders of the Moghuls was Babur, who in 1520 led the first Moghul raids into India. By 1526 he had founded the Moghul empire in India.

Babur had a grandson called Akbar, who became leader of the Moghuls when he was only 13 years old. Akbar built up an empire by conquest that finally included all of northern India.

The Moghul empire in India

Akbar was interested in more than fighting. He encouraged the work of painters, poets and musicians as well as the studies of the **scholars** at his court. He also wanted his empire to be peaceful and worked hard to make it so.

The main problem in the empire was one of religion. The people of India were **Hindus**, who worshipped their own gods. The Moghuls were **Muslims** who followed the religion of Islam. What was the best way to get the two religions to live in peace together?

Akbar found some of the answers. The highest posts in his government were given to Hindus as well as to Muslims, and he put an end to the special taxes that Hindus had been forced to pay. Akbar also married a Hindu princess.

In 1569, Akbar built his capital city at Fatehpur Sikri because his sons had been born near there. A wall ran round three sides of the city, and there was a huge lake on the fourth side. Inside the wall there were royal palaces, including one for Akbar's wife. There was also a magnificent temple, or mosque. The gateway of the mosque is still thought to be one of India's greatest architectural works.

◀ The Moghul emperor Babur receiving visitors in his garden. The Moghuls made ornamental gardens around their palaces, and enjoyed resting in them.

▲ When Akbar's son, Murad was born at Fatehpur Sikri everyone was happy. The mother shows her son off at the top of the picture, while underneath astrologers predict his future.

The Moghuls after Akbar

When Akbar died in 1605, his son Jahangir became emperor. Jahangir was not interested in governing properly, and under his rule quarrels broke out between Hindus and Muslims. He also spent the wealth of the Moghul empire on unnecessary **luxuries** instead of for the good of the people.

During Jahangir's reign, traders began to arrive from Britain and Portugal, and the first British **ambassador** was appointed to the Moghul court.

The Taj Mahal

Jahangir's son Shah Jahan became ruler on his father's death in 1627. Shah Jahan's reign is known for its magnificent architecture. The most well-known structure of the period is the Taj Mahal, which the emperor had built as a tomb for his favourite wife, the Empress Mumtaz.

Both Shah Jahan and his son Aurnagzeb who followed him as emperor were very intolerant of non-Muslim religions. Under their rule, Hindus were no longer allowed to worship their own gods, and Aurnagzeb even put one religious leader to death.

People objected to the new laws, which included an increase in taxes, and Moghul power in India was weakened. Gradually the Moghul empire in India came to an end.

▼ It took 20 000 labourers 18 years to build the Taj Mahal. The structure was completed in 1648.

Empires in the New World

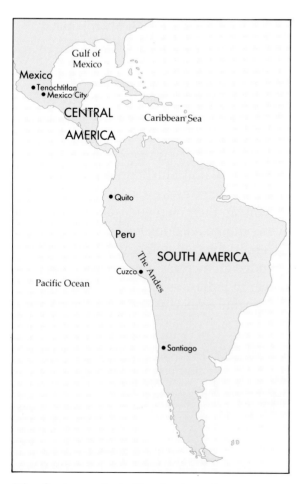

The first people to live in America came from Asia nearly 30 000 years ago. They probably crossed in the far north, because at that time Asia and America were joined by a land bridge at what is now the Bering Strait.

Many of these early people lived a nomadic life on the plains of North America, where the land was so rich in animals and fruit that they had no need to settle and farm. They became the American Indians.

Not all the tribes stayed on the plains, however. Some moved south to become the first civilizations in South America. The earliest ones that historians know about were the Aztecs in Mexico and the Incas in Peru.

In Europe and Asia, ideas were carried from one place to another by travellers and soldiers. American civilizations could not learn from others because they were cut off from the rest of the world. They had to find out everything for themselves.

The Maya and the Toltecs

About 5000 years ago, people began to settle in the valleys of Central America. One group, the Maya, lived in the area that is now Guatemala. The Maya were farmers, and their main crop was maize, which they dried for storage and ground into flour. Although the Maya were not interested in trade or in conquering other tribes, a Mayan civilization began to grow. It was at its height between AD 300 and 900.

In some ways the Mayan civilization was similar to the one that had developed 5000 years earlier in Egypt. The Maya invented both writing and counting systems, and a calendar to help them plan their farming. The calendar had 365 days like ours, but it was divided into 18 months of 20 days each. The five days left over were considered to be very unlucky. The Maya were less advanced than the Egyptians. They did not discover the wheel, and they did not learn how to make tools from iron.

No one knows exactly why the Mayan civilization ended. It may have been a natural disaster such as an earthquake. It is

▲ The temple at Chichen Itza in Mexico. The city was founded by the Toltecs using Mayan labour.

more likely, however, that they were conquered by the next empire builders, the Toltecs, who ruled in Mexico from AD 1000 to 1200.

The Toltecs took over a number of small states by defeating them in battle. They were warriors, but they were good builders and skilled craftworkers. Metalworking was introduced under their rule.

The Toltec empire ended when it was invaded. Among the invaders was the Aztec tribe, who started to build an empire in Mexico in the fifteenth century.

▶ In the mountainous parts of Peru, terraces were cut into the hillsides to make the land easier to farm.

The Sun people

Little is known about the early history of the Incas, except from their traditional stories. The first Inca ruler, Manco Capac, is said to have come out of a cave in the mountains to lead a group of people on a journey which lasted several years. This group moved from village to village in search of fertile land and at last, in about 1200, they settled in Cuzco, high in the Andes mountains.

At Cuzco the settlers built a capital city and formed the civilization that grew into the Inca empire. From Cuzco, the Incas attacked and conquered the tribes that lived along the shores of the Pacific Ocean. By 1500 AD, the Inca empire stretched thousands of kilometres from north of Quito in the country which is now Ecuador to south of Santiago in the area which is now covered by Chile.

The Inca empire

The Inca people worshipped the Sun as their god. They believed that their leader was carrying out the Sun's orders and that they had to do exactly as he told them. This meant that all the people of the Inca empire were slaves. They were told where to live, what to wear, when to work and when to rest. Everyone had to work for a time in the mines or on roads.

The only person who owned anything was the emperor, and everything in the Inca empire belonged to him. Parents could not even think of their children as their own, for children were often taken away from home to work.

▲ The Incas were skilled craft workers. This wooden drinking vessel has been made in the shape of a jaguar's head.

The Inca empire, however, was run in a well-ordered way. Food was stored in case of a bad harvest, so that everyone always had enough to eat. The government also made sure that people who were blind, crippled or handicapped in some way did not have to starve because they could not work.

Well-made roads covered the empire, with rest-houses where government officials could stay. Where roads had to cross rivers, the Incas built bridges woven from climbing plants. They also organized a system of runners to carry official messages from one end of the empire to the other.

The end of the Incas

In 1531, the Incas saw the first people they had ever seen from the outside world, when the Spanish army landed on the Pacific coast, near Quito. The Spaniards, who were led by Francisco Pizarro, were armed with guns and cannons and could move quickly on horseback. The Incas had only spears, and they stood no chance at all.

The Spanish army made good use of the Incas' roads to move quickly. One city after another was destroyed, and Atahualpa, the Inca chief, was captured and killed. Any Incas who could get away escaped into the mountains. In a few years almost all signs of the Inca empire had vanished. The people themselves did not disappear, however. Descendants of the Incas are still to be found in Peru, and they still speak Quechua, the language that was used throughout the Inca empire.

▼ The fortress of Sacsayhuaman was built above Cuzco, the central city of the Inca empire.

▼ The ruins of Machu Picchu, high in the Andes mountains. The city was discovered in 1912 by the American archaeologist Highram Bingham.

The last emperor of the Aztecs

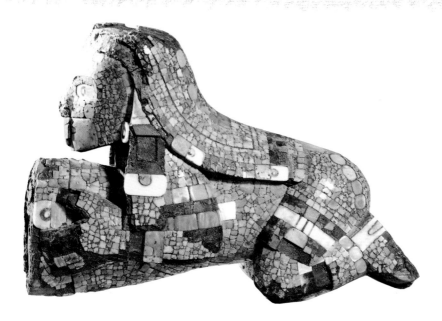

◀ The handle of an Aztec knife, covered with a mosaic of turquoise.

When the Aztecs first came to Mexico from the north in the 1200s, they were poor and did not own any land. They built a village of reed huts on an island among the marshes around Lake Texcoco, near the place which is now Mexico City.

The Aztecs built up small islands from the mud of the marshes and the lake floor, and used these islands for growing crops. This was called 'chinampa' or 'floating garden' agriculture, and it made the Aztecs successful.

By 1325, their village had grown into Tenochtitlan, a magnificent city of temples and pyramids. It had wide streets and large squares, and a regular supply of fresh water from the mountains. From Tenochtitlan, which the Aztecs had made their capital city, they became the leaders of Mexico in the 1400s. They ruled an empire that stretched as far south as the countries that are now Honduras and Nicaragua.

War and expansion

The head of every Aztec household in Tenochtitlan had to serve for a certain amount of time in the Aztec army. This meant that there was a well-trained army ready to fight at any time. The army was equipped with weapons which were edged with obsidian, a natural glass which could be made very sharp.

The Aztecs had two reasons to attack other states, First, the cities they conquered had to pay tribute in prized goods such as metal, jade and turquoise, as well as cotton, cacao, or cocoa, feathers and animal skins.

Secondly, the Aztecs needed prisoners for **sacrifice**. The most important thing in the life of the Aztecs was their religion. They believed that their duty was to fight and die for their gods. They also believed that the end of the world might come at any time, and it could be delayed only by sacrificing humans to the gods. The long flights of steps that led down from Aztec temples had a purpose. At the top, people were killed in sacrifice to the gods, then their bodies were thrown down the steps.

In 1502, a new emperor called Montezuma II came to the throne. He was a priest as well as a ruler, and he believed that everything that happened had a meaning.

Soon after Montezuma II became the ruler of the Aztecs, the temple at Tenochtitlan caught fire. There were terrible thunderstorms, and one night a comet appeared in the sky. For Montezuma, these events meant that the world was about to end, and more human sacrifices were needed to stop it happening.

He sent his army out to conquer new lands and bring back more prisoners. Thousands of people were sacrificed because Montezuma believed it was the only way to save the world.

▲ The 'Stone of the Sun', weighing 25 tonnes, once stood in the Great Temple in Tenochtitlan. It was used as a calendar. The face in the centre is the sun god.

The Spanish conquest

In one way, Montezuma was right, the Aztec world *was* about to come to an end. In 1521, Tenochtitlan was attacked by an army of Spanish soldiers, led by Hernan Cortes.

When the attack came, Montezuma climbed up to the roof of his palace and told his people to make peace. The crowd below were angry and threw stones at him. Some hit Montezuma's head and three days later he died.

The Spanish army had horses, armour, steel swords and guns, whereas the Aztecs had only their glass-edged swords. Tenochtitlan was conquered and destroyed. The Aztec empire was at an end.

◄ The chinampas, or floating gardens, built by the Aztecs in the 1200s.

Time chart

Date	Europe, Australia, New Zealand	Asia	Africa	North, Central and South America
BC 8000		The first settlements near the Nile, Tigris and Euphrates rivers		
5000		The first settlements near the Yellow River in China		
3500		The building of the first cities of Sumer		
3000		The Assyrians settle in the Assur hills		The beginnings of Mayan settlement in Central America
2500		The first settlements in Indus Valley		
2340		Sargon becomes king of Akkad		
2230		The end of the Akkadian empire		
1792		Hammurabi becomes ruler of Babylon		
1503			Hatshepsut becomes queen of Egypt	
1500		The Shang dynasty rules China		
1492			Hatshepsut's expedition to Punt	
800			Carthage founded as Phoenician colony	
750	Greek colonies are established around the Mediterranean Sea			
730		The Assyrian conquest of Babylon and building of Nineveh		
668		Ashurbanipal becomes king of Assyria		
612		The destruction of Nineveh		
600			The beginning of Carthaginian empire	
530		The Persian empire grows in size and strength		
529		Cyrus of Persia killed in battle		
521		Darius the Great becomes king of Persia		
334		Alexander the Great invades Persia		

Date	Europe, Australia, New Zealand	Asia	Africa	North, Central and South America
330		Alexander the Great invades India		
272		Ashoka becomes king of Maurya		
264	War breaks out between Rome and Carthage			
232		Death of Ashoka		
221		Shih Huang Ti becomes emperor of China		
218	Hannibal's march begins			
210		Death of Shih Huang Ti		
202			Hannibal is defeated by Scipio	
60	Julius Caesar joins First Triumvirate to rule Roman Empire			
55	Caesar is murdered			
AD				
43	The Roman invasion of Britain			
434	Attila becomes king of the Huns			
451	Attila attacks Gaul			
453	Death of Attila			
1200				The Inca empire is founded
1206		Genghis Khan becomes the khan of the Mongols		
1227		Death of Genghis Khan		
1260		Kublai Khan becomes leader of the Mongols		
1325				The Aztec capital, Tenochtitlan, is founded
1500				The Inca empire is at its peak
1502				Montezuma II becomes emperor of the Aztecs
1521		Babur founds the Moghul empire in India		
1531				Spanish invasion of the Inca empire
1556			Akbar becomes leader of the Moghuls	
1605			Death of Akbar	

Glossary

ambassador: a high-ranking official who represents the interests of a country and its people in a foreign country

archaeologist: a person who studies historical remains to gain information about ancient history

campaign: a series of planned battles within a period of time or geographical area

citizen: a male member of Greek society who was allowed to vote

city state: a Greek city with its own ruler and government

civil war: a war between members of the same country, rather than between different countries

civilization: a group of people who have settled in one place to live. They have rules and laws about the way they live and behave

colony: a group of people who settle away from their own country, but still consider that they belong to it and are part of it

cuneiform: a form of writing with letters made of wedge-shaped marks

dowry: the money, land or goods a woman brings with her when she marries. This custom still exists in some parts of the world

dynasty: a series of rulers who all come from the same family

expedition: an organized journey which is made for a special purpose, such as to find out about other lands

fertile: a word used to describe land that is good for growing crops

Gallic: the word used to describe someone or something which comes from Gaul

government: a group of people who run, or govern, a city or country and make its laws

Hindu: a follower of the Hindu religion which is based on more than one god and a belief in re-birth. Hindus believe that the way people live one life affects the sort of life they will be re-born into

irrigate: to supply water to dry land so that crops can be grown on it. The water is usually taken from a nearby stream or river or from under the ground

luxury: something that is bought for pleasure, rather than because it is needed

Muslim: a follower of the Islamic religion which is based on the teachings of the Prophet Mohammed

nomad: a person who moves about from place to place in order to find food or grazing for animals

peninsula: a piece of land which is surrounded by water on three sides

prophet: a person who teaches about a religion, claiming their knowledge has been passed on to them directly from a god

relay: a team of runners or riders who take over from each other at different stages of a race or journey

republic: a country or part of a country which is ruled by its people through their chosen representatives

retreat: the action of an army moving away from an enemy or withdrawing from a battle

sacrifice: the killing of a person or an animal as an offering to a god

satrap: a section of the Persian empire

scholar: a person who spends time studying and learning

senate: the assembly of men who ruled the Roman Empire

succeed: to take over the leadership of a country or empire from the previous ruler

tax: a payment which the people of a country must make to their government. Taxes pay for the running of a government and all the services that it provides

tolerant: allowing people to express themselves freely without fear of punishment, regardless of the beliefs and opinions they hold

trade: to do business by buying and selling goods

triumvirate: a joint rule by three men

warrior: a soldier who is involved in or who has had experience of a war

Index